ISBN

Hardcover: 978-1-969733-43-7
Paperback: 978-1-969733-42-0

This booklet is dedicated to people who want more for breakfast.

This booklet is NOT meant for beginner's cooks.

Breakfast was my favorite meal of the day since younger age. Growing up, even though I savored my mom's delicious fresh Mediterranean lunche. I always dreamed and wished we had breakfast all day long!

I do not consider this book as a recipe book or a cookbook but rather hints for variety of breakfast ideas!

As a health-conscious person, I always strived to choose fresh, healthy foods and ingredients that bring many health benefits to my being.

I am sharing these breakfast hints hoping that you use these ingredients more often to your diet, ingredients rich in natural fibers and essential vitamins, such as Omega-3 fatty acids vitamins C, D, and B, and more. Low-carb foods that support brain function heart health, and overall well-being.

After all, you are what you eat!

Enjoy!

FRENCH TOAST

FRENCH TOAST. BANANA. CAROB MOLSSAES.

Ingredients per person:

1. 1 banana cut in rounds.
2. French toast prepared as per package's directions.
3. 1 Tbsp. of carob molasses.
4. 1 Tbsp. of tahini sauce
5. 1 Tbsp. of pistachios.
6. 1 Tbsp. sesame seeds.

Prepare French toast as per the package's directions, smear on a plate a mix of the tahini sauce and carob molasses together. Add the cooked French toast on top of the sauce, add the bananas, pistachios. Sprinkle all with sesame seeds.

Enjoy!

FRENCH TOAST. PASTRY CRÈME. BERRIES.

Ingredients per person:

1. French toast prepared & cooked following the package's directions.
2. Pastry crème prepared as per package's directions. Or custard.
3. 1 Tbsp. of mixed berries.
4. 1 Tbsp. of pistachios.
5. Drizzle of honey.

Prepare & cook the French toast following the package's directions.

Drizzle honey on a plate, place the cooked French toast on top, add a couple of pastry crème's scoops or custard. Sprinkle pistachios and the mixed berries.

Enjoy!

FRENCH TOAST. CACTUS. YOGURT.

Ingredients per person:

1. French toast prepared following the package's directions.
2. 2 slices of cactus fruit.
3. 1 Tbsp. of pistachios.
4. 5 Dried yogurt balls (found in a Mediterranean grocery store).
5. Honey drizzle or maple syrup.

Drizzle honey or maple syrup on a plate, place the cooked French's toast on top, add the cactus fruit. Sprinkle all with the pistachios. Roll a few yogurt balls. Add honey to taste.

Enjoy!

FRENCH TOAST. FETA. BERRIES.

Ingredients per person:

1. French toast prepared following package's directions.
2. 1 Tbsp. of crumbled Feta cheese.
3. 3 Tbsp. of berry sauce. Blueberries or mixed berries.

To make the berry sauce:

Add a whole bag of frozen berries to a pot, cover berries with water halfway, add 4 diced dates. Let the berry mix boil and simmer. Stir it from time to time until water is half evaporated from pot. Mash few of the berries, boil again for few minutes and it's done!

Prepare the French toast following the package's directions. Spread the berry sauce on a plate, add the French toast to it and the crumbled Feta cheese goes on top of all.

Enjoy!

FRENCH TOAST.
AVOCADO.

Ingredients per person:

1. French toast prepared following the package's directions.

2. 1 avocado mashed.

3. 1 Tbsp. of pomegranate seeds.

4. Drizzle of honey or maple syrup.

Prepare & cook French toast following the package's directions.

Drizzle the Honey or Maple syrup on a plate. Add the 2 scoops of mashed avocado on top of French toast. Top all with the pomegranate seeds.

Bon Appetit!

GRAINS. BEANS. DAIRY.

GRANOLA. BERRIES.

Ingredients per person:

1.   4 Tbsp. of berry sauce.
2.   2 Tbsp. granola of your choice.
3.   1 Tbsp. of pistachios.
4.   4 pitted and sliced dates.
5.   2 Tbsp. of mango puree' (mango to be blended in an electrical blender until smooth).

To make the berry sauce: Add a whole bag of frozen berries to a pot, cover berries with water halfway, add 4 diced dates. Let the mix boil, simmer and stir from time to time until water is half evaporated from pot. Mash the berries, boil again for few minutes and it is done!

Assemble all the ingredients in a bowl together.

And enjoy!

GRANOLA.
CUSTARD.

Ingredients per person:

1. 1 Cup of already made vanilla custard (follow package's directions)
2. ½ Cup of granola, your choice.
3. ¼ Cup of dried red berries or any dried berry or raisins.

Assemble all ingredients together.

Enjoy!

AVOCADO.
LENTILS.
YOGURT.

Ingredients per person:

1. 1 avocado, a half for each person
2. ¼ Cup of boiled lentils prepared following the package's directions.
3. 2 Tbsp. of Greek yogurt.
4. 1 Tbsp. of olive oil.
5. Pinch of salt, pepper, and paprika.

Place yogurt over the half avocado. Place the cooked lentils over the yogurt. Then drizzle the olive oil on top of all.

Sprinkle it with salt, pepper, and paprika.

Enjoy!

CHEESE. TOMATO.

Ingredients per person:

1. 1 sliced, grilled medium size tomato.
2. 2 thin slices of cheddar or gouda cheese.
3. 1 Tbsp. of pitted green olives.
4. 1 Tbsp. of olive oil.
5. 3 or 4 yogurt balls (found in Mediterranean grocery stores).
6. Pinch of salt & pepper.

Place the cheddar cheese on top of the tomatoes while they are still on griddle. Once the cheese is melted, place all on a dish, sprinkle the pitted olives and yogurt balls. Drizzle the olive oil. Add pinch of salt & pepper to taste.

Enjoy!

YOGURT. PISTACHIOS. WALNUT.

Ingredients per person:

1. 1 cup of Greek yogurt
2. 1 Tbsp. of roasted or raw pistachios.
3. 1 Tbsp. of roasted or raw walnut.
4. 1/2 Tbsp. of olive oil.
5. Pinch of paprika or hot pepper to taste.

In a cup, add the yogurt. On top of that, add both walnut and pistachios, then add the olive oil. Sprinkle the paprika or hot pepper to taste.

Enjoy!

YOGURT.
TANGERINE.

Ingredients per person:

1. 1 cup of Greek yogurt.
2. 1 tangerine sliced in rounds, grilled then peeled and diced.
3. 1 Tbsp of toasted shredded coconut.
4. 1 Tbsp of raw or roasted pistachios.
5. 1 Tbsp. of honey.

In a bowl add the yogurt and then add the sliced peeled tangerine, then add the pistachios and coconut. Drizzle all with honey. Enjoy!

14

BANANA. YOGURT.

Ingredients per person:

1. 1 banana cut lengthwise and grilled.
2. 1 Tbsp. of raw or roasted pumpkin seeds.
3. 1 Tbsp. of black raisins.
4. 1 Tbsp of black honey or maple syrup.
5. Drizzle of olive oil.
6. 2 Tbsp. of Greek yogurt.

Over heated griddle, drizzle the olive oil and grill the bananas until you see brown marks.

Transfer bananas to a dish, add the yogurt. Spread the raisins on top, add the pumpkin seeds. Drizzle the maple syrup or the honey.

Enjoy!

RED BEANS. CHEESE.

Ingredients per person:

1. ½ a cup of boiled & strained red beans.
2. 1 Tbsp. of pitted green olives.
3. ¼ of shredded Mozzarella cheese.
4. Pinch of salt & pepper.
5. One egg.
6. Shredded half of an onion is optional.

Mix the strained cooked beans with the egg & onions.

Blend all with an electrical blender until smooth. Form patties from mixture, grill the patties on a griddle until brownish red color, add cheese on top. Grill for few min more until cheese is melted.

Sprinkle the olives over patties in a dish, drizzle all with olive oil. Add salt & pepper to taste.

Enjoy!

APPLES. FETA.

Ingredients per person:

1. 1 apple cut in half. Roast the apple around 40 minutes, covered with a foil until is soft and brown marks is on it.
2. 1 Tbsp. of crumbled feta cheese.
3. 1 Tbsp. of pistachios.
4. 1 Tbsp of diced walnuts.
5. Drizzle of black honey or maple syrup.
6. Drizzle of olive oil.
7. Salt & black pepper to taste.

Drizzle the olive oil over the already cut in half apple. Add pinch of salt and black pepper. Roast apple in an oven covered for 40 minutes, covered with a foil until is soft and brown marks is on it, then uncover the last 4 minutes.   Plate the baked apple, add the crumbled feta cheese on top, then add pistachios, walnuts and honey.

Bon Appetit!

POTATOES. CHEESE.

Ingredients for 2 persons:

1. One head of half boiled potatoes.
2. 1.5 cup of shredded mozzarella or Cheddar cheese.
3. Pinch of salt & pepper.

Sprinkle ½ a cup of the shredded cheese at the bottom of a silicone baking dish. The dish size 25 cm x 15 cm

Slice the potatoes in half thick slices. Layer one row of potatoes on top of cheese, sprinkle salt & pepper, spread another layer (1/2 cup) of cheese on top of potatoes.

Add a 2nd layer of potatoes on top of cheese, salt & pepper then top it with the remaining ½ a cup of cheese. Cover the dish, bake for 40 minutes. Uncover the dish the last 4 minutes. Bake for extra 4 minutes or until cheese is melted and have reddish color. Wait for it until it's cool before slicing it.

Enjoy!

RED BEANS. POMEGRANATE.

Ingredients per person:

1. ½ a cup of boiled strained red beans. Follow the package's directions.
2. One egg.
3. 2 Tbsp. of pomegranate molasses.
4. 1 Tbsp. of pomegranate seeds.
5. Pinch of salt & pepper to taste.

Add the egg to the cooked, strained red beans in a bowl, mix all with an electrical blender, add to the mixture 1 tbsp. of the molasses, salt & pepper. Mix all until smooth.

Form patties from mixture and grill until you see griddle marks.

Place patties on a dish. Drizzle all with the remaining 1 tbsp. of the molasses. Sprinkle the pomegranate seeds on top.

Enjoy!

CHICKPEAS. YOGURT. EGGPLANT.

Ingredients per person:

1. ½ Cup of boiled & strained chickpeas. Follow the package's directions.
2. 6 Thinly sliced small eggplants covered with foil, roasted with 2 tbsp. of olive oil, salt & pepper for 25 minutes.
3. 2 Tbsp. of Greek yogurt.
4. 1 Tbsp. of olive oil.
5. Pinch of salt & pepper.
6. 1 clove of mashed garlic is optional.

Place the thinly sliced roasted eggplant on a dish, place the chickpeas mixed with the mashed garlic in the middle.   Yogurt goes on top of Chickpeas.   Drizzle all with olive oil. Sprinkle salt & pepper to taste.

Enjoy!

EGGS

EGGS.
EGGPLANT.

Ingredients per person:

1. 2 Eggs.
2. 1 Tbsp. of semolina flour.
3. 1 Tbsp. of granulated mustard.
4. 2 Tbsp. of olive oil.
5. Pinch of salt & pepper.
6. Pinch of paprika or hot pepper.
7. One small eggplant sliced thin.

Roast the thin sliced eggplant in 2 tbsp of olive oil with salt and pepper in an oven dish covered for around 25 min.

Brush the bottom of a cupped pan with the remaining olive oil. Sprinkle the semolina flour. Add one egg per cup, place the eggplant on top. Cook egg until it's done.

Smear the mustard on a dish, place the eggs on top. Sprinkle paprika or hot pepper.

Enjoy!

CABBAGE. EGGS.

Ingredients per person:

1. 2 Eggs.
2. One thick slice of roasted cabbage in a heated from top & bottom oven. Drizzle the cabbage with little bit of olive oil. Roast it covered for 50 minutes.
3. 1 Tbsp. of crumbled feta cheese.
4. Around 4 cornichons pickles.
5. Pinch of salt & pepper.
6. 2 Tbsp. of olive oil.

Add olive oil to a heated pan, fry the eggs, add the cabbage while eggs are halfway cooked.

Once eggs are done, place eggs/cabbage in a dish, sprinkle the cheese on top. Add cornichons pickles. Then add salt & pepper to taste,

Enjoy!

EGGS. ROASTED VEGGIES.

Ingredients per person:

1. 2 Eggs.
2. Roasted Veggies: 2 small thin sliced eggplants, ¼ head of cauliflower florets. 1 small head of thin sliced sweet potatoes. All veggies are roasted in an oven dish covered with 2 tbsp. of olive oil, salt & pepper for 45 minutes.
3. Drizzle of olive oil.
4. Walnut stuffed eggplant pickles with hot pepper (found in Mediterranean stores).
5. 1 Tbsp. of shredded mozzarella cheese.

While the 2 eggs being cooked in a heated pan with the olive oil, add the roasted vegies, continue cooking eggs until is done, sprinkle the cheese on top.

When cheese is melted, transfer the eggs/veggies on a plate, placed the pickled stuffed eggplant on top.

Enjoy!

EGGS.
ARTICHOKE.

Ingredients for 2 persons:

1. 3 eggs.
2. 1 Tbsp. of pitted olives.
3. 1 medium size tomatoes sliced in half rounds.
4. 1 medium size white shredded onion.
5. ½ a green pepper cut in rounds.
6. 3 artichoke hearts halved.
7. 1 Tbsp. of olive oil.
8. 1 cup shredded mozzarella or cheddar cheese.

Sprinkle ½ a cup of the cheese in a silicone oven dish. Line the green peppers rounds on top of cheese. Line the artichoke hearts on top of peppers. Crack an egg over each artichoke heart. Line up the tomatoes on the sides of the cheese. Sprinkle the salt and pepper. Add the remaining cheese on top.

Cover and roast in an oven on medium heat covered for 25 minutes. Uncover the last 4 minutes. Dish will be done when you see reddish marks on cheese. Spread the olives over the plated cheese. Wait until it cools before slicing it.

Enjoy!

EGGS. TOMATOES. AVOCADO.

Ingredients per person:

1. 2 Eggs.
2. 1 Tomato sliced in rounds, grilled.
3. 2 Thick slices of one small avocado.
4. 2 Tbsp. of shredded mozzarella or cheddar cheese.
5. 2 Tbsp. of olive oil.
6. 2 Tbsp. of semolina flour.
7. Pinch salt, black pepper, paprika or hot pepper to taste.

Brush 1 tbsp. of olive oil in each of the 2 cups placed in a heated pan,, sprinkle the semolina evenly into these 2 cups. Place one slice of avocado in each cup, top the avocado with one slice of grilled tomatoes slice for each cup. Crack one egg for each cup on top of the veggies.

Cook until is done. Add the cheese, salt and pepper. Move the eggs cups into a plate smeared with olive oil & paprika or hot pepper.

Enjoy!

EGGS. ONIONS.

Ingredients per person:

1. One white onion cut in rounds.
2. ½ a green pepper diced
3. 2 Eggs.
4. 2 Tbsp. of semolina flour.
5. 2 Tbsp. olive oil.
6. Salt & pepper to taste.

Place the olive oil in a heated pan. Sprinkle the semolina flour. Warm it a little bit then add the onions rounds, let them fry little, when they welt and little brown/ red, add the beaten 2 eggs. Eggs can be beaten or whole.

Add the diced green pepper when eggs are halfway done. Add pinch of salt & pepper to taste. Sprinkle again 1 tbsp. of semolina flour on top then flip all the mix. Only once. Wait couple of minutes and is done!

Enjoy!